Where Is
New Jersey?

Where Is
New Jersey?

by Tracy Vonder Brink and Annette Whipple

illustrated by Ted Hammond

Penguin Workshop

To all readers who celebrate
curiosity—TVB and AW

PENGUIN WORKSHOP
An imprint of Penguin Random House LLC
1745 Broadway, New York, NY 10019
penguinrandomhouse.com

Designed and Produced by Dinardo Design, LLC.

Library of Congress Cataloging-in-Publication Data is available.

First published in the United States of America by Penguin Workshop, 2026

Manufactured in the United States of America
CJKW

ISBN 9798217053315 (paperback)
10 9 8 7 6 5 4 3 2 1

ISBN 9798217053322 (library binding)
10 9 8 7 6 5 4 3 2 1

The authorized representative in the EU for product safety and compliance is Penguin Random House Ireland, Morrison Chambers, 32 Nassau Street, Dublin D02 YH68, Ireland, https://eu-contact.penguin.ie.

Contents

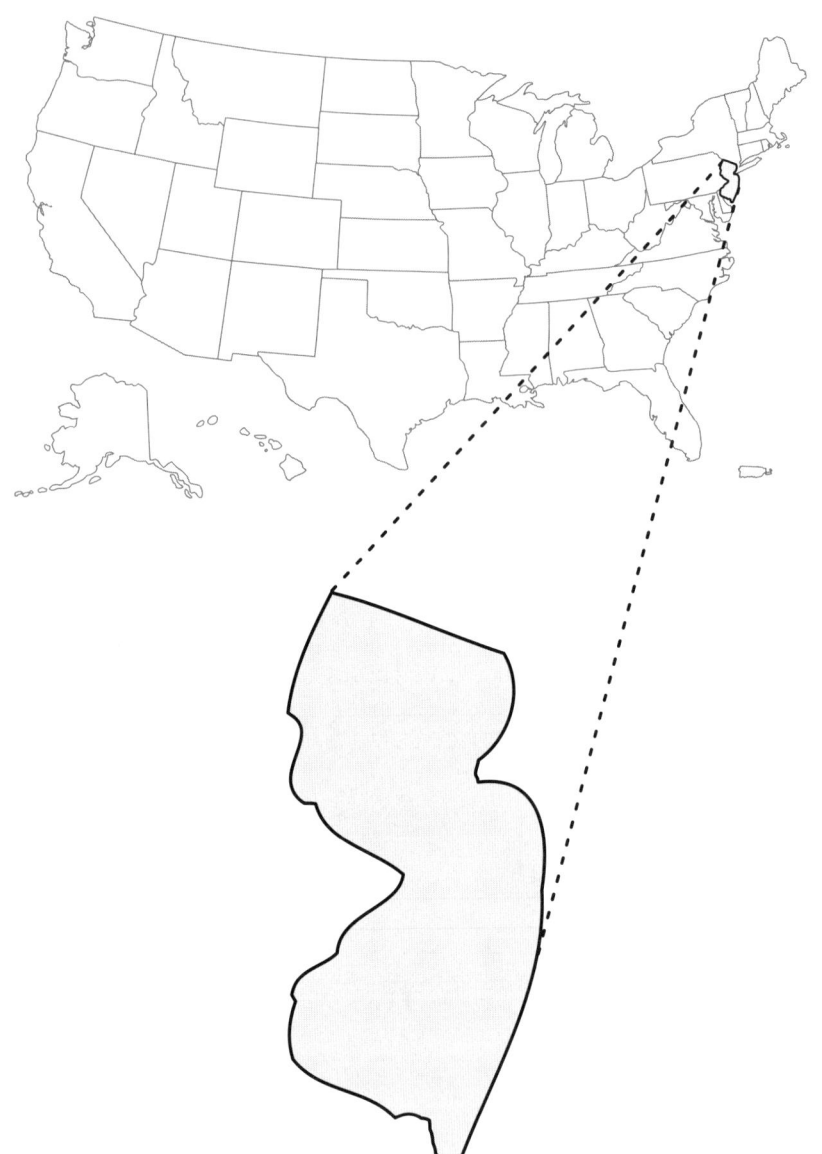

Where Is New Jersey?

Thomas Edison was a full-time inventor from the age of twenty-two. Starting in 1876, Edison and his team worked together in a laboratory in Menlo Park, New Jersey, where they used scientific equipment for experiments. Edison called it the Invention Factory. In 1877, he had an idea for a machine that could record spoken messages. Edison drew a design for the recording machine and gave it to one of his team members to build.

Soon, the machine was ready. Edison turned a wheel on its side and yelled into a mouthpiece, "Mary had a little lamb . . ." Then he turned the wheel back to the starting point. To his amazement, he heard his voice saying the nursery rhyme! "I was never so taken aback in my life," he said later, astounded at what he had heard.

Edison called his invention the phonograph. He and his workers built more and showed them off to the public. The president of the United States even invited Edison to the White House to demonstrate his invention.

The phonograph wasn't the last big invention created in the state. Edison is one of many New Jerseyans who have helped change the world.

CHAPTER 1
Welcome to New Jersey

The small state of New Jersey includes farmland and mountains as well as cities and suburbs. It has a history of firsts with new products, services, and events. Though it covers less than nine thousand square miles, the state is known for its diversity—in land, animals, people, and life.

New Jersey is located on the East Coast between Philadelphia and New York City. The state is considered a peninsula because water surrounds it on three sides. The Atlantic Ocean provides about 125 miles of shoreline, including towns with beaches where people go on vacation, such as Atlantic City, Cape May, and Ocean City. The Hudson River runs between New Jersey and New York, and the Delaware River separates it

from Pennsylvania and Delaware.

The people of New Jersey enjoy four distinct seasons. Summer in New Jersey is often hot and humid, so locals and tourists refresh themselves at the shore. Colorful leaves on trees brighten New Jersey's landscape in fall until the cold sets in for a snowy winter.

The changing weather creates habitats for

many animals. Marshes, swamps, and ponds are home to spring peepers and other frogs. Milk snakes live in forests and fields. Forests cover nearly half the state and are home to black bears, coyotes, and wild turkeys. Many bobcats used to roam throughout New Jersey. They're only found in wooded mountains in the northwestern part of the state. The bobcat is now endangered, which means there are so few left that they need protection to survive. Marine animals, including humpback whales and leatherback turtles, live off the Jersey Shore in the Atlantic Ocean.

The land of New Jersey has also been home to people for thousands of years. The Lenni-Lenape (say: LEN-ny lun-NAH-pay) were the largest Indigenous nation in the land that we now call New Jersey. (They're often called the Lenape Nation as well as the Delaware Nation.) Their name means "original people" in their language.

The Lenape farmed, fished, and hunted. They caught clams offshore. They also made clay pottery. One pot has been found that was large enough to cook two white-tailed deer in!

The Lenape included many smaller groups, such as the Powhatan Renape (say: POW-uh-tan run-NU-peh) and Ramapo Munsee Lenape. There may have been as many as twenty thousand

Lenape people in New Jersey at the beginning of the 1600s.

Henry Hudson was the first European to come into contact with the Lenape people in this area in 1609. He traded knives and beads for tobacco. Hudson claimed land for the Dutch people and called it New Netherlands. The nearby river was soon known as the Hudson River.

During the 1600s, settlers from the Netherlands, Sweden, and Finland began arriving in what is now New Jersey. They traded with one another as well as with the Lenape people. Animal pelts (or skins), such as those of beavers, were used in Europe to make hats and could be sold for a lot of money.

As time went on, the European settlers spread out. They took more land from the Lenape people, and violence arose. Willem Kieft (say: KEEFT), the governor of New Netherlands, wanted to make money by taxing Indigenous people. When some hogs went missing from a plantation in the Dutch settlement New Amsterdam, soldiers wrongly accused and killed Lenape men, women, and children from the Raritan group across the river. The Raritans fought back.

By 1660, the Dutch had created their first permanent European settlement. Just a few years later, the British (also called English) controlled the land. The British divided the land into West Jersey and East Jersey.

Freedom of religion and low land prices attracted more European settlers to West and East Jersey. Many immigrants followed the Quaker religious movement. Quakers believe all people are equal and should live peacefully, without war. Quakers settled West Jersey and focused on religious freedom and equality. Religion was also important in East Jersey, but the people there paid more attention to building businesses.

During this time, the local Lenape population shrank. Many died from diseases the Europeans had brought with them. Some Lenape left the area and joined other Indigenous nations in Pennsylvania and New York. Those who remained had their land taken by the government for settlers.

West Jersey and East Jersey came together as

one British colony, New Jersey, in 1702. About fourteen thousand people in New Jersey shared a governor with the colony of New York. Many European settlers lived along the shore and fished. In other parts, large family farms of more than one hundred acres grew crops such as vegetables and flax, a plant used to make fabric and oil. Food and animals from farms, as well as lumber (wooden boards), were sent to Philadelphia and New York City, which had previously been named New Amsterdam.

The colony of New Jersey thrived. By 1760, nearly one hundred thousand people lived there. Cities such as Elizabethtown, Trenton, and New Brunswick became leading business centers.

Farming continued with the forced labor of enslaved workers. Some immigrants brought enslaved African people when they came to the colonies. Others purchased enslaved people in New York City. Most worked on large farms, particularly in East Jersey. Some colonists were against slavery, but many were enslavers. About ten thousand enslaved people were forced to work in New Jersey in the late 1700s.

The British king required the colonists to pay high taxes but didn't give them any say in the government. The colonists wanted a voice, but the king ignored them. Many agreed they needed to separate from Britain. That meant war.

The American Revolution began in 1775 in Massachusetts. Five New Jersey representatives signed the Declaration of Independence when the British colonies in America united to announce they were a new country: the United States of America. New Jersey's location was important during the war. To its north was New York, where the British army often camped. To its west was Philadelphia, which had been named the capital of the United States.

George Washington was the general of the

Continental Army for the United States. His troops spent more time in New Jersey than any other state. Washington tracked the British army's movements in New York City from New Jersey. American soldiers foraged, which means they found food growing in the wild. Morristown shops supplied Washington's troops with weapons.

The army moved to different states to fight the British. On December 25, 1776, General Washington and his troops left Pennsylvania while it was still dark. They crossed the partially frozen Delaware River in shallow boats and arrived in Trenton, New Jersey, before dawn. The early attack surprised the German troops who were working with the British. Washington's soldiers surrounded the city. It was their first victory!

Several days later, Washington's army won an important battle in Princeton. Before these victories, the US Army had little hope of winning the war. The Battles of Trenton and Princeton gave the soldiers the confidence they needed to win the war.

Many colonists supported the fight for independence, but some stayed loyal to Britain. Mixed support, a central location, and all the battles within its borders earned New Jersey a nickname: the Crossroads of the American Revolution.

The American Revolution ended in 1783. New Jersey had over one hundred battles and saw more fighting on its soil than any other state.

New Jersey was the third colony to agree to the new country's constitution in 1787. It was officially a state! Trenton became the state capital where local governmental decisions were made.

CHAPTER 2
Early New Jersey

As the United States grew, New Jersey's population grew, too. In the early 1800s, many people in the state still farmed and sold crops, such as peas, tomatoes, and berries. There were also jobs in factories that made and sold items to use.

New ways of travel changed New Jersey. As railroad tracks crossed more land, trains shipped products outside of the state. Trains also carried people to travel in a short amount of time. Human-made rivers, called canals, allowed ships to reach more cities. Public boats, called ferries, could carry many people across the water. Ferries helped New Jerseyans reach Pennsylvania and New York to work or sell their goods.

Paterson's rivers and waterfalls made it a perfect location for many businesses. Rushing water-powered mills and rivers made it easy to send products to other towns. Steam trains and weapons were made there. By the late 1800s, Paterson was known as Silk City because nearly half of all silk fabric made in the United States was made there.

More European immigrants arrived in New Jersey. They worked in factories, small businesses, and on farms. Black people (both enslaved and free) worked alongside them. An 1804 law made buying an enslaved person illegal in New Jersey, but children born to enslaved people were not born free. Some tried to escape slavery with the help of the Underground Railroad. This was a secret group that helped Black freedom seekers find food, shelter, and information on their way north to Canada, where slavery was illegal.

William Still was a free Black man born in

New Jersey in 1821. He secretly worked to help many freedom seekers on the Underground Railroad. He also reconnected Black families who had been separated. In 1850, Still was working in an office in

William Still

Philadelphia when a man visited looking for help. The man, called Peter, wanted to find his family. Peter had been born in Philadelphia but was later enslaved in Alabama. After decades of enslavement, he bought his freedom and made his way north. Peter didn't know if he should trust the man in the office. But Still knew who Peter wanted to find—because Peter was his long-lost brother! Together, they crossed the Delaware River so Peter could be united with their elderly mother in New Jersey. Still helped more than six hundred freedom seekers and was called the Father of the Underground Railroad.

Digging for Dinosaurs

In Haddonfield, New Jersey, John Estaugh (say: es-TAW) Hopkins found some huge bones while digging on his farm in the 1830s. They fascinated him, so he displayed them in his home and showed them to curious friends and family. Hopkins may not have been able to guess when the animal lived or what kind of animal the bones were from since at the time, most people didn't know much about fossils (remains from animals that lived long ago).

In 1858, his friend William Parker Foulke visited for dinner. Hopkins showed the amateur geologist (a scientist who studies rocks) the strange bones. Foulke may have wondered what other fossils were buried on the farm. Hopkins gave permission for scientists to look.

More dinosaur bones were found. One bone was four feet long. The scientists estimated the dinosaur

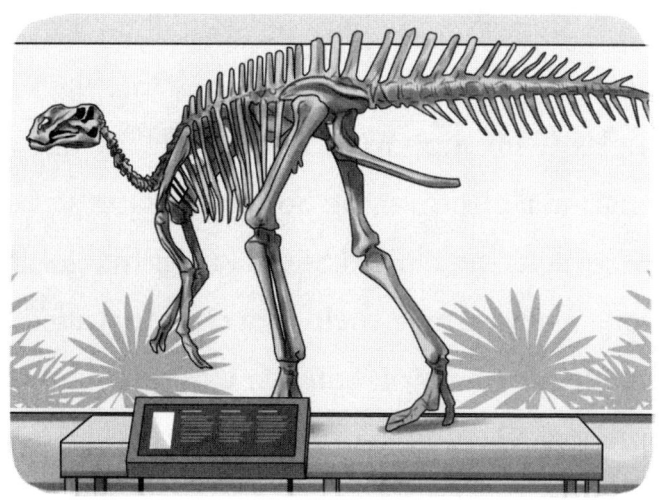

called *Hadrosaurus foulkii* would have been about twenty-five feet long and weighed up to four tons! *Hadrosaurus foulkii* was the most complete dinosaur skeleton found in North America at the time and one of the first to be studied. Scientists think this duck-billed dinosaur, with the name that means "Foulke's Big Lizard," ate plants and walked on four legs most of the time. Until this discovery, scientists didn't know that some dinosaurs could walk upright.

In the presidential election of 1860, the New Jersey vote was split between Abraham Lincoln (who was against slavery) and Stephen A. Douglas (who supported it). When Lincoln won the national election, the Southern states seceded from, or left, the United States rather than outlaw slavery. They formed their own country called the Confederate States of America (also known as the Confederacy). The Northern states were called the Union.

The two countries began fighting the Civil War in 1861. New Jersey was close to both nations. Many white people in the state supported slavery, and some still enslaved people. Others made a lot of profit from sending products to the South. Though not everyone in the state agreed, New Jersey fought on the side of the Union.

More than seventy thousand men from New Jersey served in the war. This included almost three thousand Black men who fought as US

Colored Troops. Some women helped as military nurses. A New Jersey woman named Dorothea Dix oversaw nurses in the Union Army. She hired thousands of nurses. Still, more than five thousand soldiers from New Jersey died in the war.

When the Civil War ended in 1865, the United States became one nation again. Slavery was outlawed in the South. New Jersey was the last state in the country to outlaw slavery on January 23, 1866.

Across the United States and especially in the South, violence and unfair laws still made life difficult for Black people. Many moved north, including to New Jersey. Atlantic City became one destination for Black families because it offered lots of work in the service industry. They built communities and businesses, especially in the Northside neighborhood.

Atlantic City became a popular place for city

residents to vacation along the ocean. People traveled by train and boat to the shore town. With fewer people and more fresh air than New York City or Camden, Atlantic City was seen as a relaxing place to visit in the 1870s. Tourists walked along the beach, ate in fancy restaurants, and shopped in stores. They rented wool bathing suits that covered their whole bodies to swim in the ocean. But having the town just steps away from the beach led to a problem: sand.

When local businesses were concerned about the sand tracked into their shops, the city created an elevated sidewalk made of boards eight feet wide. It was called the Boardwalk. Soon, the city tried something never done before: They built a pier over the ocean. For ten cents, visitors watched acts such as the escape artist Harry Houdini on the pier. Houdini could break out of handcuffs, locked boxes, and coffins—even underwater!

New Jersey wasn't just known for relaxing. It

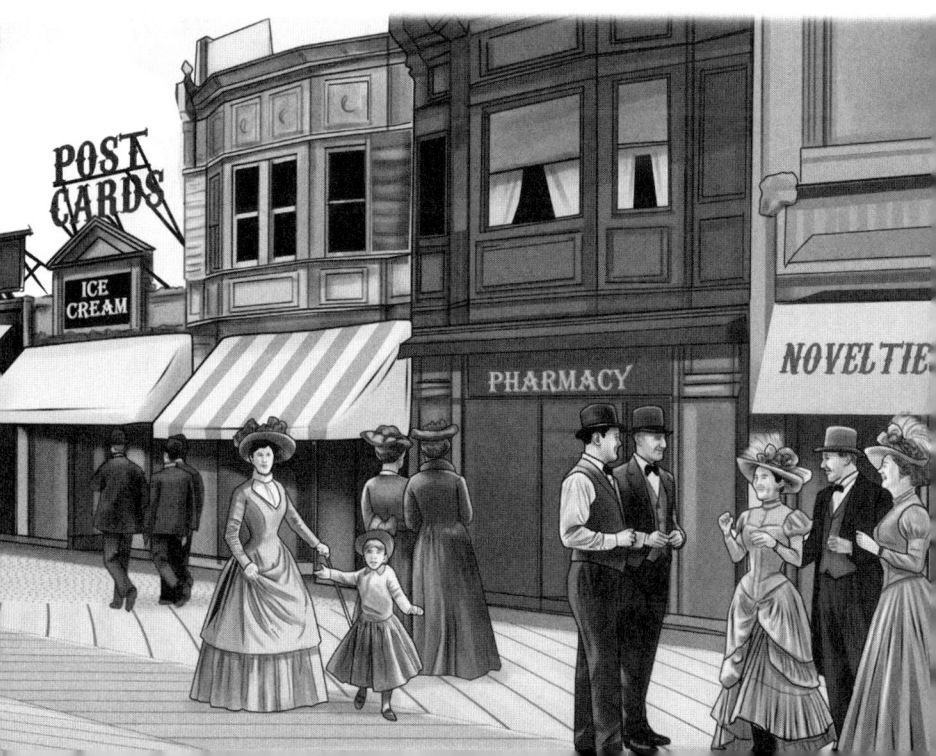

was also a center for scientific research. After the phonograph, Thomas Edison invented the first commercial light bulb. Electric lights changed the way people lived, since they could work, read, or simply see clearly after dark without having to burn oil lamps or candles. Later, Edison and his team filmed *The Great Train Robbery*. The ten-minute silent black-and-white film helped launch the movie industry.

New medical research was important, too. A company founded by three brothers in New Brunswick, called Johnson & Johnson, focused on health care. At the time, cotton used in surgery wasn't made in a clean way. The Johnson brothers knew gauze (woven cloth used to cover wounds) would be safer. They developed sterile cotton made in flat sheets. It was a breakthrough in medicine. New Jersey would see more medical breakthroughs in the future.

CHAPTER 3
Growth and Change

Thanks to the food grown there, New Jersey had been called the Garden State since the mid-1800s. In the 1900s, a new crop was added—blueberries! At that time, most farmers believed wild blueberry bushes were too difficult to grow. Farmer Elizabeth Coleman White thought differently. She worked with scientist Frederick Vernon Coville, who studied blueberries and the kind of soil they needed to grow. Together, they developed the first farmed blueberry bushes in 1916.

White noticed fancy candies wrapped in a thin, see-through material called cellophane. She used it to cover her boxes of blueberries so shoppers could see the berries. Blueberries became an important crop for farmers in New Jersey and twenty-five other states.

Another New Jersey berry grower not only helped make canned cranberry sauce popular but also founded a hugely successful company. In 1917, Elizabeth Lee sold the first canned cranberry sauce in the state. She teamed up with two other cranberry growers in Massachusetts and formed Cranberry Canners, Inc. Lee was the new company's vice president. She was also nicknamed the Queen of Cranberries. Later, the company was renamed Ocean Spray.

New Jersey governor Woodrow Wilson became president of the United States in 1913. World War I broke out in Europe a year later. Wilson wanted to keep the United States out of the war, but Germany sank more and more ships, including American ones. In 1916, German agents blew up railroad cars filled with weapons on Black Tom Island in Jersey City. Four people were killed. Less than a year later, the United States entered the war.

New Jersey became an important staging area (a place where soldiers and equipment are gathered and prepared). Two million US troops passed through Camp Dix, Camp Merritt, and other training camps in the state. More than 140,000 New Jerseyans served in the war, including New Jerseyans who became part of the first Black regiment to fight in World War I.

When the war ended in 1918, many Americans were ready to have fun. Atlantic City became known as the Nation's Playground. Families enjoyed carousels and other rides in amusement parks along the Boardwalk. By 1923, as many as three hundred thousand people visited Atlantic City every day in the summer. Atlantic City's piers had theaters where visitors could watch plays and musicals before the shows headed to New York City. Tourists also packed nightclubs to listen to jazz music in the coming years, played by performers such as legendary New Jerseyan Count Basie.

In 1928, travel to New Jersey became even easier when Newark Airport opened. It was the first airport in the United States with a concrete runway for planes to take off and land. The United States Post Office declared Newark Airport "the most important airport in the world." Amelia Earhart set a record when she flew from Los Angeles to Newark, making her the first woman to complete a nonstop, cross-country flight completely on her own.

New Jerseyans continued to come up with new ideas. Around 1920, Earle Dickson wanted to make a bandage his wife could use if she cut herself while cooking. The bandages they had at home were too big. He took tape, gauze, and fabric and made a small bandage his wife could stick on by herself.

Dickson worked at Johnson & Johnson, and he showed his invention to his bosses. They called it the Band-Aid.

Around the same time, Sarah Spencer Washington owned a hairdressing business in Atlantic City. She also taught students there. Washington noticed not many hair care products were made for Black Americans. She founded

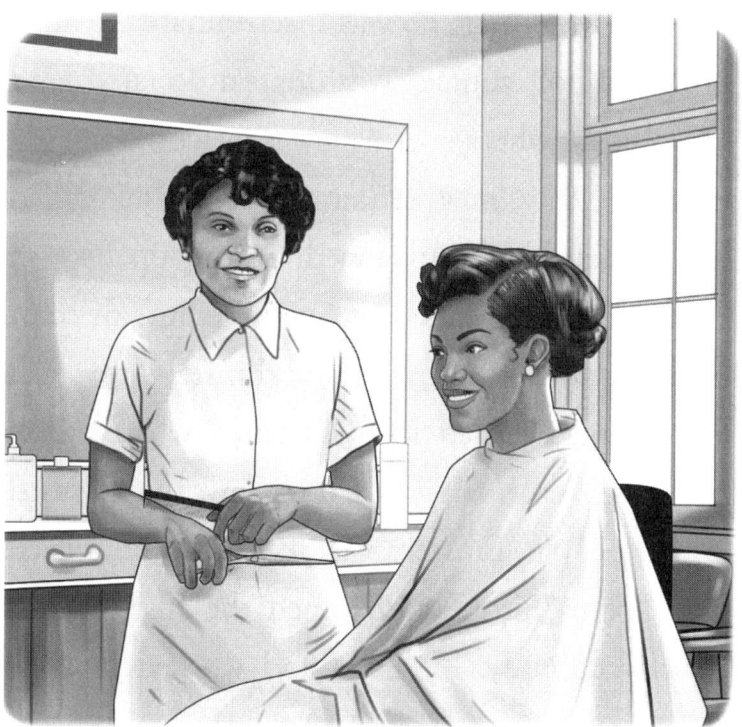

the Apex News & Hair Company to change that. Her company made seventy-five different products that were sold around the world. Washington also opened beauty schools in twelve states. Washington became one of the first Black woman millionaires. She gave back to her Atlantic City community. She gifted land for a children's camp and opened a nursing home for the elderly. When she was discriminated against at a local golf course, Washington donated land for a course where everyone was welcome.

In 1930, a new center for scientists, called the Institute for Advanced Study, opened in Princeton. Two years later, the institute's director asked famous scientist Albert Einstein to teach there. Einstein had left Germany, where Adolf Hitler's government was making laws that harmed Jewish people. Einstein was Jewish, so he moved away from Europe and joined the Institute for Advanced Study. He lived and worked in New

Jersey for the rest of his life.

Other important scientists followed, including some who were escaping Europe the way Einstein did. Women scientists also joined the

Institute for Advanced Study because many other universities at that time didn't allow women in their programs. Discoveries made by Einstein and other scientists at the institute led to the development of computers and new ideas about how the universe works. Today, it's still one of the country's leading research programs.

Tragedy struck in the New Jersey skies in 1937 when the German airship *Hindenburg* came in for a landing. The eight-hundred-foot airship was made of fabric stretched over an aluminum frame and filled with hydrogen gas (which is lighter than air) to make it float. On the evening of May 6, the *Hindenburg* burst into flames as it tried to land at the Naval Air Station in Lakehurst. A spark had caused the hydrogen gas to catch fire. The airship burned up in less than a minute. Thirty-six people died. Reporters captured the fire on film, and the *Hindenburg* accident became one of the most famous disasters in history.

In 1939, Adolph Hitler's German army invaded Poland. Within a few years, Great Britain, France, and the Soviet Union were fighting Germany, Italy, and Japan in World War II. The United States stayed out of the conflict until 1941 when Japan attacked the US naval base in Pearl Harbor, Hawaii. New Jersey again became a staging area for war.

Three million soldiers passed through training camps in New Jersey. More than 560,000 New Jerseyans served in the war. Shipyards in Hoboken built and repaired ships. A battleship named after the state was launched in 1942. The USS *New Jersey* went on to travel more miles and fight in more battles than any battleship in United States history. Today, the *New Jersey* is permanently anchored as a museum on the Delaware River near Camden.

Before World War II, many New Jerseyans lived in cities. After the war, companies built houses

in communities outside of cities, called suburbs. Soldiers coming home from the war moved to the suburbs to start families. The New Jersey Turnpike opened in 1951, making it easier for people to live in the suburbs and drive to work in the cities. It was one of the country's first modern highways. More than 17 million vehicles drove the 118-mile turnpike the first year it was open. Later, it grew to cover 148 miles and became an important route linking Washington, Baltimore, Philadelphia, and New York City. More than 200 million vehicles now drive it every year!

A year after the turnpike opened, a scientist named Selman Waksman (say: WAX-man) won the Nobel Prize for a life-saving discovery in medicine. A disease called tuberculosis was so deadly that, at one point, it killed more than four hundred Americans per day. Waksman worked at Rutgers University and studied soil. He thought microbes (very small living things) in soil might make medicines that could fight diseases. His thinking led him and his team to discover the first treatment for tuberculosis. Waksman's work also led to the development of at least twenty other medicines.

At Bell Labs, scientists had created the transistor, a small device that controls the flow of electric currents in items such as radios. Transistors became the building blocks of all modern electronics—we wouldn't have computers, cell phones, or televisions without them. Lasers were invented at Bell Labs in the 1950s. In 1962, Bell Labs and NASA (National Aeronautics and Space Administration) even launched the first satellite that transmitted TV signals!

Over time, New Yorkers who wanted homes and offices realized New Jersey was much cheaper than New York City. The area along the Hudson River, called the Gold Coast, became especially popular in the 1980s. About four million square feet of office space was built and at least three thousand homes. Construction boomed in other parts of the state, too. New Jersey became a place where many wanted to live and work.

CHAPTER 4
The Great State of New Jersey

New Jersey is the fourth smallest US state, but it's the most densely populated (meaning that a lot of people live close together). More than nine million people live in its 7,354 square miles of land. That's 1,259 people for every mile! Newark is its largest city. More than 300,000 people live there. The Gold Coast continues to be a popular place where many live and work.

The state recognizes three Indigenous nations—the Nanticoke Lenni-Lenape Tribe, the Ramapo Lenape Nation, and the Powhatan Renape Nation. The Nanticoke Lenni-Lenape Tribe is the largest in the state, with most members living in southern New Jersey. The Ramapo live in the foothills of the Ramapo mountains on the border of New York and New Jersey. The Powhatan Renape are based in Rancocas. Members of these nations work to bring attention to their history and hope to open a museum about their culture.

New Jersey is home to thirteen of the world's top twenty companies that make medicines. Big tech companies, such as Samsung Electronics America and LG Electronics North America, are headquartered in New Jersey. It's home to more scientists per square mile than any other state! Researchers from Rutgers and Princeton Universities have won fifty Nobel Prizes for their work.

The Garden State also has more than nine thousand farms that bring in billions of dollars every year. Its farmers grow more than one hundred kinds of fruits and vegetables. New Jersey is one of the nation's top three producers of cranberries, peaches, and bell peppers. It's also one of the top five blueberry growers. The famous Jersey tomato was developed in 1934 when scientists from Rutgers University and Campbell's Soup teamed up to make a tasty tomato that could be grown almost anywhere. In 2016, Rutgers and Campbell's Soup released a new tomato related to the one developed in 1934. The Rutgers 250—named after the university's 250th anniversary—quickly became a hit.

More than 120 million people visited New Jersey in 2024. Tourists spend time in Atlantic City and on the Jersey Shore's beaches. For a sweet treat, visitors enjoy saltwater taffy. The sticky, stretchy candy was invented in Atlantic City. For a meal, they might eat in one of the hundreds of diners (an affordable restaurant that serves American food) that make New Jersey "the Diner Capital of the World." It has also been ranked as the best pizza state, with more than two thousand pizzerias!

To hike, bike, canoe, and camp, some visitors and New Jerseyans head to the New Jersey Pinelands. This area covers more than one million acres and is made up of thick pine and oak forests and swampy wetlands. The Pinelands include Pinelands National Reserve (a natural

area protected by the government). It was the first national reserve set aside in the United States. People sometimes have fun scaring themselves with stories about the Jersey Devil, a creature that's said to roam the Pine Barrens.

Hunting for fossils is another New Jersey activity. Fossils have been discovered in nineteen of the state's twenty-one counties. Visitors who look for fossils in the Poricy (say: POR-uh-see) Park Fossil Beds may take home up to five. Ancient shark teeth can be found in the streams in Big Brook Park. In 1991, *Hadrosaurus foulkii* was made the state dinosaur after students from Strawbridge Elementary School in Haddon Township spent four years writing hundreds of letters to the state government.

New Jerseyans also enjoy music. Famous singers Frank Sinatra, Sarah Vaughan, and Whitney Houston were from New Jersey. So are rock musicians Jon Bon Jovi and Bruce

Springsteen, both of whom still live in the state. New Jerseyan Paul Robeson was not only a singer on Broadway and in the movies but a four-sport athlete and the first Black man to play football for Rutgers. He also became a pro football player.

Sports have a long history in the state. The first baseball game, the first professional basketball game, and the first American football game were all played in New Jersey! Today, the New York Giants and the New York Jets National Football League teams both play at MetLife Stadium in East Rutherford. The New Jersey Devils National Hockey League team plays in Newark and has won three Stanley Cup Championships. Track-and-field superstar Carl Lewis, one of only four Olympic athletes to have won nine gold medals, grew up in Willingboro. The Los Angeles Angels picked baseball star Mike Trout to play for them after he graduated from Millville High School in New Jersey.

Carl Lewis

Millions of people make their homes in New Jersey. Millions more visit its cities and coast. Its crops are enjoyed around the country. Ideas and inventions from its people and companies have changed the world. New Jersey isn't the biggest state, but it plays a big part in the United States.

New Jersey at a Glance

Statehood: 1787

Nickname: The Garden State

Abbreviation: NJ

State Motto: Liberty and Prosperity

State Tree: Red oak

State Animal: Horse

Capital: Trenton

Size: 8,723 square miles

Population: Over 9 million

Famous People from New Jersey:

Halsey (singer), Judy Blume (author), Edwin "Buzz" Aldrin (astronaut), Ice-T (rapper, actor), Queen Latifah (actress, singer, rapper)

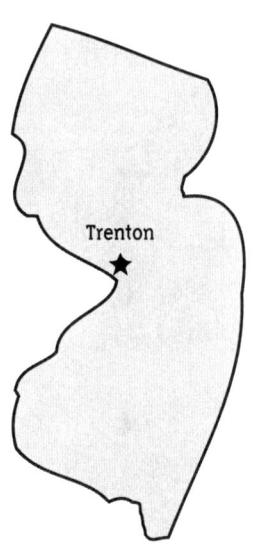

State flag

State bird
Eastern goldfinch

State flower
Violet

FUN FACT:

The first-ever drive-in theater, where people could watch movies from their cars, opened in Camden in 1933.

Timeline of New Jersey

1609 — The Lenape people trade with Henry Hudson

1660 — The Dutch create first permanent European settlement

1702 — West Jersey and East Jersey unite to form the British colony of New Jersey

1776 — The Battle of Trenton is the first American victory in the American Revolution

1787 — New Jersey becomes the third US state

1866 — New Jersey outlaws slavery

1879 — Thomas Edison invents the commercial incandescent light bulb

1886 — Health-care company Johnson & Johnson is founded

1920 — Atlantic City is known as the "Nation's Playground"

1928 — Newark Airport opens

1930 — The Institute for Advanced Study opens in Princeton

1943 — The treatment for tuberculosis is discovered at Rutgers University

1951 — The New Jersey Turnpike opens

1978 — Pinelands National Reserve is set aside

1991 — *Hadrosaurus foulkii* named the state dinosaur

2024 — More than 120 million people visit New Jersey

Timeline of the World

1610 — Italian astronomer Galileo discovers the first four moons of Jupiter

1643 — Louis XIV becomes king of France

1703 — Russian ruler Peter the Great founds the city of Saint Petersburg

1778 — France secretly agrees to supply the United States during the American Revolution

1783 — The Montgolfier brothers fly the world's first hot-air balloon in France

1868 — Russia sells Alaska to the United States

1879 — The first underwater cable between South Africa and Europe is launched

1918 — Women over age thirty gain the right to vote in Great Britain

1928 — Penicillin is discovered

1930 — Mickey Mouse appears in a comic strip for the first time

1946 — The first computer is introduced

1951 — China takes control of Tibet

1978 — The first spam email is sent

1991 — The world's first website is launched

2024 — Summer Olympics and Paralympics are hosted in Paris, France

Bibliography

*Books for young readers

Frith, Margaret. *Who Was Thomas Alva Edison?* New York: Penguin Workshop, 2005.

Grack, Rachel. *New Jersey*. Minnetonka, MN: Bellwether Media, 2022.

"New Jersey." *Britannica Kids*. kids.britannica.com/kids/article/New-Jersey/345507.

"New Jersey Pictures and Facts." *National Geographic Kids*. kids.nationalgeographic.com/geography/states/article/new-jersey.

Pascal, Janet B. *What Was the Hindenburg?* New York: Penguin Workshop, 2014.

Sabol, Stephanie. *Who Is Bruce Springsteen?* New York: Penguin Workshop, 2016.

"A Short History of New Jersey." NJ.gov. nj.gov/nj/about/history/short_history.shtml.

"Symbols." NJ.gov. nj.gov/nj/about/symbols/.

*Tate, Don. *William Still and His Freedom Stories: The Father of the Underground Railroad*. Atlanta: Peachtree, 2020.

Walsh, Helen Evans. *New Jersey*. Minneapolis: Abdo Publishing, 2023.